The How to Write Book

A step-by-step guide to writing friendly letters and business letters, book reports, formal reports, essays, poetry and short stories

Written by Ellen Hajek
Illustrated by David Helton

Teaching & Learning Company

1204 Buchanan St., P.O. Box 10
Carthage, IL 62321-0010

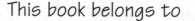

This book belongs to

_____

Cover art by David Helton

Copyright © 1999, Teaching & Learning Company

ISBN No. 1-57310-187-7

Printing No. 987654321

Teaching & Learning Company
1204 Buchanan St., P.O. Box 10
Carthage, IL 62321-0010

Table of Contents

Dear Teacher or Parent,

This book is designed to help your elementary students build confidence as well as skill. Students who have had limited success in writing are often fearful of new assignments and may become so uptight that they cannot think creatively or logically. Specific features of this book such as page styling with plenty of open space, clear wording, easy-to-follow instructions and models for every major assignment help to insure that your students will be relaxed and able to work effectively.

The book is laid out to encourage the students to think before they write, and to organize their ideas into a clear, readable piece. In Step 1, they learn to brainstorm for ideas and to group ideas into paragraphs. Step 2 encourages them to write using a specific format. Step 3 takes the students through the steps of writing a formal report including research, writing and proofreading. The final section, Step 4, reviews ways to use nouns, verbs and modifiers to make writing more interesting. It also reviews compound and complex sentences and offers assignments in creative writing.

"Just for Fun" activities in each section encourage the students to use the creative side of their brains. These activities help them recognize that words are tools and to learn that they have command over them. Answers for "Just for Fun" as well as for other exercises are in the back of the book.

I hope that you and your students find the activities in this book to be fun as well as educational. Above all, I hope that your students learn to enjoy writing.

Sincerely,

Ellen

Ellen Hajek

STEP 1
Using Your Noodle

Writing Is Thinking

The first and most important step of any writing project is thinking about the message you want to give your reader. Because thinking is so important, we need to understand how messages work in our brains.

Scientists tell us that the human brain has two halves—one half to create ideas and the other to figure out how to put those ideas to use. We get the idea in the right brain and then move the idea to the left brain to figure out how to use it.

Most writers find that they cannot create when they feel stressed or under pressure. They say it helps to just relax, take a walk, stretch or just do some deep breathing. Relaxing helps the creative side of the brain to function properly.

Writing is a very powerful form of communication. When you speak, the person who hears your words receives them only once. However, when you write, your words can be reread several times. In order to get exactly what you want to say across to your reader, you must keep three questions in mind: Who are you? Who will read your work? What do you want to say?

Who Are You?

This does not just mean that you should know your name! It also means that you should know what your relationship is to the reader. Are you writing a letter to your grandmother, or are you writing a request to a business for information? What is important about you to your grandmother–your health, your happiness, what you are doing? What is important to a business?

Who Will Read Your Work?

Is it someone you know well, or is it someone you would like to impress? How does that person want to be treated? Is there anything you can say that will help that person feel that you are truly thinking of him or her and not just anyone?

What Do You Want to Say?

If you are writing a friendly letter, you probably just want to tell what has been happening at your house. If you are writing a report, you want to give special information.

Name _____

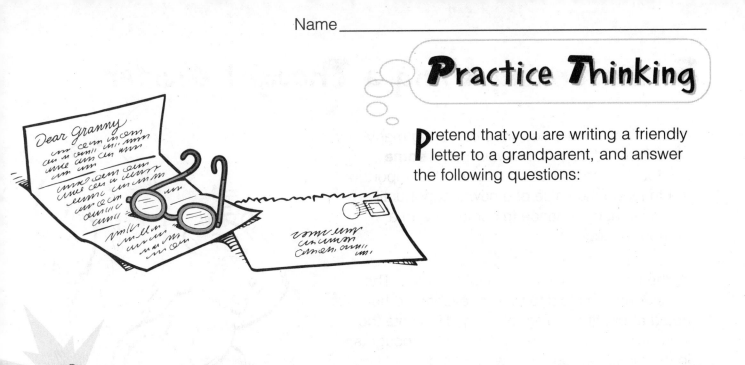

Pretend that you are writing a friendly letter to a grandparent, and answer the following questions:

1. Who will read your writing? _____

2. What should that person know about you?

_____

_____

_____

_____

_____

3. What is one thing that you want to say? _____

_____

_____

_____

Brainstorming Using a Thought Cluster

Thinking about a new idea can bring many different thoughts into your mind–**some useful** and others **not so useful**. It is important not to judge the value of a new thought until you have had a chance to come up with a number of choices.

The pattern below is a thought cluster. The student was told to think of everything he could about the subject of trees. He wrote the word *trees* in the center and wrote his thoughts in the clouds around the center word.

After the student had written **several choices**, he used only those that would help him to write his assignment.

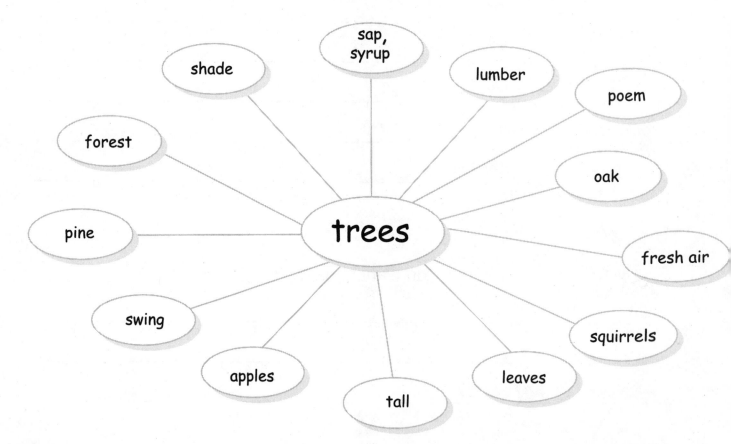

Practice Using a Thought Cluster

In the space below, make a thought cluster for the word *friends*. Don't spend a lot of time thinking about your choices. Just write the **first words** that come into your mind.

Grouping Your Ideas

Some of the ideas in a thought cluster are closely related. You can find the ones that have a relationship and make a statement that ties them together. For example, the words from the sample thought cluster could be grouped under sentences such as the following:

Example 1

Trees are beautiful.
forest
poem
leaves
squirrels

If you were to write about each of the words in this group and how they are related to the sentence, you might say something like . . .

> "I think that trees are beautiful. I love to see the way the leaves move in the breeze, and I like to watch squirrels jump from branch to branch. Someday I may write a poem about how beautiful trees are."

Example 2

Trees are important for food and shelter.
shade
apples
fresh air
sap, syrup
lumber

If you were to write about this group of words, you might say something like . . .

> "Trees are important for food and shelter. Many kinds of trees produce foods like apples and maple syrup for us. The leaves of trees give us shade in the summer and also help to clean the air we breathe. Some trees give us lumber for houses and buildings."

Now it's time to switch to the left side of your brain. Deciding which ideas fit together and what topics you want to include takes lots of brainwork! Take the thoughts from the cluster that you just did and look at them. What thoughts seem to be related? What general statement can you make that shows the relationship?

Notice that not all of the thoughts from the sample cluster were included in the groupings above. You may find that some of your thoughts do not seem to fit any of the general statements you make. In that case, just leave out thoughts that don't fit.

More Practice in Grouping Ideas

bowling

hang gliding

volleyball

sports

tennis

hiking

baseball

sports

Select ideas from the thought cluster on the left that will fit into the topics below.

I meet interesting people by playing group sports.

_____

_____

_____

I get into shape with individual sports.

_____

_____

_____

Write topic ideas for the groups of items below.

1. walking, horse and buggy, early railroad

_____

_____

2. jet plane, space shuttle, superspeed train

_____

_____

Developing Paragraphs

If you look at the text in a book, you see that groups of sentences are set off together either by spaces or by indentations. Each group of sentences is called a **paragraph**.

Every paragraph has a central idea called the **topic**, and each sentence in the paragraph says something about that **idea**.

> A paragraph is a group of sentences that develops an idea.

Example: Jerry sat proudly on the elephant. He smiled and waved to everyone, and the elephant waved her trunk at the crowd. Jerry patted the elephant's head. At last, his dream had come true!

The topic sentence is "Jerry sat proudly on the elephant." The rest of the paragraph tells what Jerry does and thinks as he is sitting on the elephant.

Notice that the beginning line of the paragraph is indented. (All paragraphs are either indented or separated by spacing or both.)

> When the topic changes or the way of looking at
> the topic changes, it is time to begin a new paragraph.

Example: When Jerry's father heard what had happened, he was very surprised. "Wow!" he cried. "I thought Jerry would be afraid to sit on an elephant!"

When the topic changed from Jerry's experience to his father's reaction, the writer began a new paragraph.

Name _____

Practice Recognizing Paragraphs

HA! HA! HO HO Hee Hee HA! HA!

Remember to begin a new paragraph whenever the **topic changes** or when **someone new** begins to **speak**.

Read the following selections. For each selection, decide where the subject changes and where a new paragraph should start. Mark the place with a slash (/).

1. One of the clowns came over and introduced himself to Jerry. The clown was wearing floppy shoes and carrying a large bucket of water. When the clown asked Jerry's name, an elephant that was standing nearby reached into the bucket with her trunk and took out the water. Then she sprayed the clown until he was wet from head to toe! After the clown left, Jerry went to the monkey cage, where the monkeys were being fed. He bought a large box of food and gave some to the largest monkey. When the other monkeys saw the food, they scrambled down from their perches and grabbed it away from the largest monkey.

2. "How much did your trip to the zoo cost?" Jerry's friend asked. "Would the money I got for my birthday be enough for everything?" "I don't know," answered Jerry, "but I'll ask my dad."

3. African elephants are the largest living animals on land. Some stand 10 to 11 feet tall at the shoulder. They may weigh several tons. The Asian, or Indian, elephants are generally smaller than African elephants. They can grow to 9 to 10½ feet tall at the shoulder.

4. Jerry's dad enjoyed seeing the bears at the zoo. He took a picture of the big grizzly bear eating, and he watched two little polar bears play in the water. The birdhouse was next to the bears. Jerry's dad took pictures of the flamingos and the penguins there.

5. Some of the birds could talk. An old green parrot kept saying, "Cracker for the pretty boy" over and over in a loud voice. "Can we buy him some crackers, Dad?" Jerry asked.

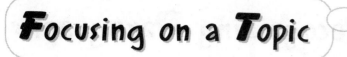

In formal writing, every paragraph has a sentence that sums up the main idea of the paragraph. We call this sentence a **topic sentence**. Although the topic sentence is usually the first sentence, it may appear anywhere in the paragraph.

Topic Sentence: When Uncle Jerry took us to the carnival Tuesday, we tried every ride.

Example: When Uncle Jerry took us to the carnival Tuesday, we tried every ride. The first thing we saw was the Ferris wheel, and we rode that twice. After that, we rode the Octopus and then the Rocket and the Speedboat. The last ride was the tamest—the merry-go-round!

When the reader sees the words *every ride*, he expects a description of each ride to follow. Every sentence in that paragraph is focused upon the topic "we tried every ride."

14

Find the Topic Sentence

F ind the topic sentence in each paragraph, and draw a circle around it.

1. Watching birds feed their babies is fun. The mother and father can hardly keep up putting worms into their children's wide-open mouths. The fuzzy babies swallow and then open up wide again.

2. Some of the best parts of a vacation don't show in the pictures you bring home. You cannot capture the sound of a waterfall or the smell of pine trees after a rain. You cannot photograph the sound of a tugboat horn or the excitement of spotting a whale in the ocean.

3. This is an excellent picture! It is clear and sharp. There is a nice balance between the child and the mountain flowers in the background. Also, the lighting is very good.

4. Sandy visited three states on her vacation. In Oklahoma, she saw Native American dancers and oil wells. In Kansas, she went to a large theater and saw a stage play. When she visited Nebraska, Sandy toured the first homestead west of the Mississippi River.

5. In the early evening, Joe heard the cries of the wild animals. Coyotes howled from their hiding places in the nearby hills. A cougar screamed, and a nearby owl gave an occasional hoot.

Name_____

Finding Topic Sentences

Find the topic sentence in each of the following paragraphs:

Examples: Everyone brought something for the picnic. Antonio brought chips and dip, and his brother Mike made sandwiches. Suzanne added homemade cookies, and Rosa brought fresh lemonade.

Topic Sentence: Everyone brought something for the picnic.

1. The wild horse bucked in every direction. First, it bucked to the left. Then it whirled around and jumped into the air. Finally, it streaked across the corral as fast as it could run.

Topic Sentence: _____

_____

_____

2. Kerri introduced Jeff to all of her relatives. First, Kerri presented her grandfather and grandmother. Then she introduced her brothers and sister. Finally, Jeff met Kerri's Aunt Lil.

Topic Sentence: _____

_____

_____

3. It rained every day for a week. The rain started on Thursday, and it came down hard. On Friday, the sun shone for a few minutes, but then the rain began again. And it rained all day every day from Saturday through Wednesday.

Topic Sentence: _____

_____

16

Writing Topic Sentences

A topic sentence has two parts—the **topic** and the **view**. The topic is who or what is doing something, and the view is the action. It tells us what they are doing.

Examples: Marta introduced us to everyone in her family.

The topic is "Marta," and the view is "introduced us to everyone in her family."

Sometimes a topic sentence also has a **clue word** that lets the reader know what to look for in the sentences that follow. In the example, the clue word is *everyone*. The reader expects to learn who "everyone" is in this family. The rest of the paragraph would probably be something like the following:

Marta's grandmother smiled and invited us to have a glass of tea. Her Aunt Sylvia shook our hands and welcomed us to the party, and her Uncle Dave just grinned and waved.

Read the following topic sentences. In each sentence, underline the topic and circle the view. Underline the clue word twice.

1. The President explained his plans.

2. Mary found four new friends.

3. Each child brought a storybook.

4. When I awakened, I saw the five children.

5. Barret gave us a tour.

Name_____

Using a Topic Sentence to Build a Paragraph

A topic sentence can come anywhere in a paragraph, but often it is the first sentence. Build a paragraph with each of the topic sentences below. You may place the given sentence anywhere within the paragraph.

1. Greg introduced us to everyone in his family.

_____

_____

_____

_____

2. Many signs warned us that a storm was coming.

_____

_____

_____

_____

18

Organizing the Information in a Paragraph

Good-bye!

Have you ever thought about what a mixed-up world this would be if we had no logical ways to do things? For example, suppose that you went to buy fruit at the grocery store. When you got to the counter, the clerk said, "Good-bye! Thank you for coming," and then he asked you for the fruit you had picked out.

When you write, give the reader some idea of what to expect by following a logical order. The most common ways to organize your thoughts are these: **spatial order, time order** and **least-to-most** (or most-to-least).

1. Use **spatial (space) order** to organize when your topic includes information about different places.

Example: Tanya wanted to see the whole island once more before she left for home. She bicycled to the beach to watch the waves slap against the rocks. After that, she rode to the top of the hill overlooking the aquarium and took several pictures. Finally, she rode to the other side of the island, where she and several friends had enjoyed a picnic.

2. Use **time order (chronologically)** to organize when your information takes place at different times.

Example: I knew that the hike would probably last about four hours. If we left home at 6 a.m., we would reach the trail by 6:30. The trail up to the overlook and back would take until 9:00, and stopping for breakfast would take us up to 10:00.

3. Use **least-to-most** when your information contains material of varying importance or different sizes.

Example: Eric knew that he could raise the money to buy a real mountain bike. He already had $15 in his savings account. He could sell his old bicycle for $50, and his paper route would bring in at least $100.

Name_____

Practice Using Logical Order

Rearrange the sentences in each of the following paragraphs into a logical order. First, identify which type of order would be best for the paragraph. Then number the sentences to show the correct order.

1. Tenisha showed her little sister how to make a snowman by using three balls of snow—one small, one medium and one large.
   Then she put the medium-sized ball on top of it.
   Finally, she put the smallest ball on the very top and added rocks for eyes.
   She rolled the large ball to a good spot on the ground.

   _____

2. Andrea gave her dog Bubbles a complete bath yesterday.
   By the time she got to the tail, he was tired of the bath and jumped out of the tub.
   She washed his face and ears with a cloth then rinsed them carefully.
   He seemed to like it when she shampooed his back and tummy.

   _____

3. Richard wanted to build a project for the science fair.
   During his second week, he planned his weather project.
   During the first week of school, he read about projects other students had built.
   From the third week until the contest, he built and tested his project.

   _____

4. Patrick went to Massachusetts last summer.
   Patrick's grandfather taught him to drive the tractor.
   They took him on a tour of their farm.
   Patrick is planning to go back again next year.
   His grandparents met him at the airport.

   _____

20

Name _____

Write Your Own Paragraph

Write a paragraph about your pet. If you do not have a pet, write about an imaginary pet. Use a topic sentence to begin your paragraph.

Example: Gordo is a very smart fish. In the morning, he watches me until I come close to his bowl. Then he gets very excited and flips his tail so that I will remember to feed him. After he eats, he swims around the bowl and makes bubbling noises to thank me for his breakfast.

_____

_____

_____

_____

_____

_____

_____

_____

_____

Name_____

More Practice Writing a Paragraph

Write a paragraph about a famous person, and have another person guess who you have written about. Remember to think about who you are and who your reader is. Then say what you want to say.

Writing a **F**riendly **L**etter

Almost everyone likes to get a letter from a friend. It is fun to have a friend share experiences and stay in touch.

Notice that Bonnie used her noodle in writing the friendly letter below. How will she answer the three important questions?

1. **Who are you?**
Bonnie is Sandy's friend from camp.

2. **Who will read your work?**
Sandy had sent pictures to Bonnie. Sandy will want to know what Bonnie thought of them.

3. **What do you want to say?**
Bonnie wants to know whether or not Sandy is coming to camp again this summer.

13,000 West 9th Avenue
Anytown, OH 00000
June 3, ____

Dear Sandy,

Thank you for sending the pictures of your horse. He is really beautiful.

I am going to the beach with my family in July. I think it will be fun to see the whales and sea lions, but I don't know if I'll like swimming in the ocean.

Are you coming to camp again this year? I hope we can bunk together again.

Are you finding any more butterflies for your collection?

Please write soon, and let me know about camp.

Your friend,

Bonnie

Writing a Friendly Letter

L et's look at Bonnie's letter again to see what the parts of a friendly letter are.

1. At the top is the **return address**, which is the address of the writer. The date goes directly below it. Sandy will need to use the return address when she writes back to Bonnie.

2. The **date** is June 3.

3. The **greeting** in this letter is "Dear Sandy."

1. → 13,000 West 9th Avenue
Anytown, OH 00000

2. → June 3, ____

3. → Dear Sandy,

4. → Thank you for sending the pictures of your horse. He is really beautiful.

I am going to the beach with my family in July. I think it will be fun to see the whales and sea lions, but I don't know if I'll like swimming in the ocean.

Are you coming to camp again this year? I hope we can bunk together again.

Are you finding any more butterflies for your collection?

Please write soon, and let me know about camp.

5. → Your friend,

6. → Bonnie

4. The **body** of a friendly letter usually includes many of the things we find in Bonnie's letter.

The first sentence refers to the last time that Bonnie heard from Sandy.

The next few sentences tell the news.

This letter also has a special purpose because Bonnie wants to know whether or not Sandy will be at camp.

The final paragraph gives direction to the reader. It lets Sandy know that Bonnie wants her to write back.

5. The **closing** is "Your friend," or whatever is in keeping with the relationship between the reader and the writer.

6. The **signature** is the name of the writer. It should always be handwritten rather than typed.

The Friendly Letter

Let's look at another example. This time, Mark is writing a thank-you note to his aunt and uncle. Write the parts of the letter in the blanks.

1. 896 Grant Street
    Anywhere, GA 00000

2. October 12, ____

3. Dear Uncle Neal and Aunt Liz,

4. Thank you for inviting me for the weekend at your house. I really had a good time riding your horse and practicing roping. The food was great, too!

    I'll send you some pictures as soon as I get them developed.

5. Love,

6. Mark

1. _____

2. _____

3. _____

4. _____

5. _____

6. _____

Name_____

Practice Writing Your Letter

On the lines below, practice writing your friendly letter. Remember to think about the three important questions and to write an ending that will let the reader know what he or she is to do. Follow the style of the letter on the previous page for placing the date, the greeting (Dear _____) and the closing (Your friend). Then copy your letter on another piece of paper and send it to your friend.

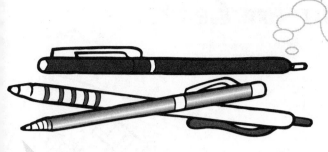

Addressing the Envelope

Study the example below. Then practice addressing an envelope to your friend. (Be sure to include the street address, city, state and zip code for each address.)

Sender's name and address →

Bonnie Kirsch
13,000 West 9th Avenue
Anytown, OH 00000

Receiver's name and address →

Ms. Sandy Kline
2400 North 50th Street
New City, OH 00000

_____

_____

_____

_____

_____

_____

It's Time to Write a Business Letter

Writing a business letter is much like writing a friendly letter because you still need to think about **who you are**, **who will read the letter** and **what you want to say**. However, a business letter is different from a friendly letter in several ways.

A business letter has an **inside address**.

The greeting is followed by a **colon** rather than a comma.

The **closing** in a business letter is formal–usually *sincerely* or *yours truly*.

The **signature** in a business letter is typed as well as handwritten.

1. Inside address

1500 Willow Lane
Anytown, CO 80666
April 12, ____

Mr. Bob Brooks
337 Overtown Road
New City, OH 87777

Dear Mr. Brooks:

Thank you for your prompt reply to my letter. I am taking your suggestion and returning the model XT radio to your shop for repair.

Would you please send me the bill when you are finished?

Sincerely,

Galen George

Galen George

2. Colon

3. Closing

4. Signature

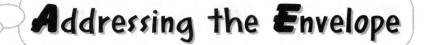

Addressing the Envelope

337 Overtown Road
New City, OH 87777
April 18, ____

Mr. Galen George
1500 Willow Lane
Anytown, CO 80666

Dear Mr. George:

Our technicians have repaired your model XT radio, and we are returning it to you by UPS. Please send a check for $31.50 for parts and labor.

Sincerely,

Bob Brooks

Bob Brooks

Bob Brooks wrote the following business letter to Galen George. Using the information in the letter, address the envelope for mailing to Mr. George.

_____

_____

_____

                            _____

                            _____

                            _____

Name_____

Practice Writing a Business Letter

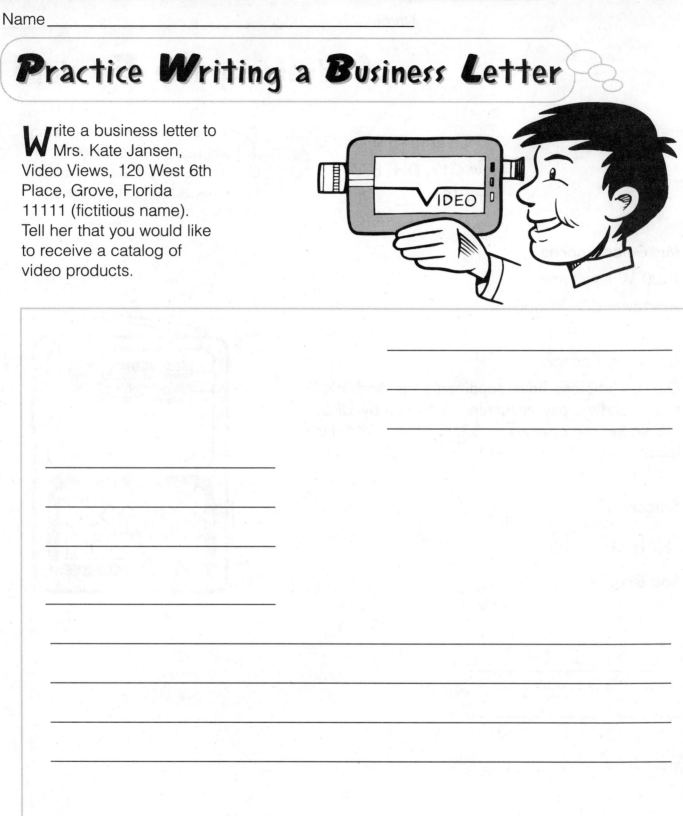

Write a business letter to Mrs. Kate Jansen, Video Views, 120 West 6th Place, Grove, Florida 11111 (fictitious name). Tell her that you would like to receive a catalog of video products.

Placing an Order

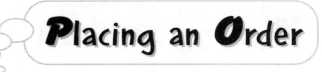

A special kind of business letter is one in which the writer is placing an order. An order must include the following information:

1. name and catalog number of each item
2. how many of each item you are ordering
3. price of each item
4. where to ship the items
5. shipping costs
6. method of payment

Catalog orders usually require payment by check, money order or credit card. It is not safe to send cash through the mail.

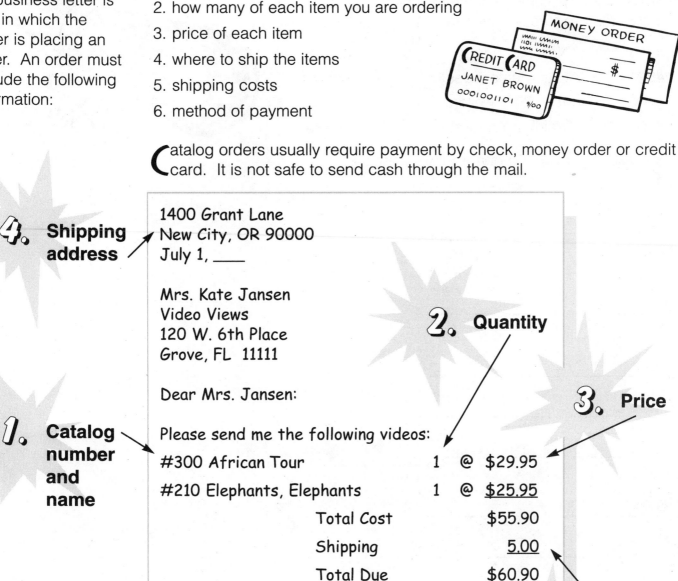

4. **Shipping address**

1400 Grant Lane
New City, OR 90000
July 1, ____

Mrs. Kate Jansen
Video Views
120 W. 6th Place
Grove, FL 11111

Dear Mrs. Jansen:

Please send me the following videos:

2. **Quantity**

3. **Price**

1. **Catalog number and name**

#300 African Tour   1 @ $29.95
#210 Elephants, Elephants   1 @ $25.95

      Total Cost $55.90
      Shipping   5.00
      Total Due $60.90

A check is enclosed for the total due.

5. **Shipping costs**

6. **Payment method**

Sincerely,

Janet Brown

Janet Brown

Name_____

Writing an Order

Choose two items from the list below, and write an order for the items to come to your house. Use the vendor's address from page 31.

#318	New Pioneers	@ $27.95
#321	Giant Telescopes	@ $25.95
#400	The Cliff Dwellers	@ $22.95
#403	Training Your Pet	@ $19.95

Please include $5.00 per order for shipping.

Name_____

Draw a line from each statement below to its correct answer at the right.

1. The first and most important step in any writing project is the _____.

2. What are the three questions you must answer when you think about writing for a reader?

3. Why should you brainstorm for ideas rather than using the first thought that comes to your mind?

4. How do you group thoughts from a cluster?

5. A paragraph is a group of sentences that develops one _____.

Arrange ideas under a main topic.

thinking

You need good ideas, and you don't want to leave anything out.

idea

Who are you?
Who is your reader?
What do you want to say?

Name _____

This business letter has blank spaces. Fill in the spaces with the terms in the box below.

greeting
return address
closing
inside address
signature
message
date
asking for a response

HMM...

1. → return address _____

_____

2. → _____

3. → _____

_____

_____

4. → _____

5. → _____

_____

_____

6. → _____

7. → _____

8. → _____

Just for Fun

Break the code to discover the message below! Each number represents the place of a letter in the alphabet. A = 1, B = 2, etc.

21, 19, 5   25, 15, 21, 18   14, 15, 15, 4, 12, 5!

34

Name_____

1. Fuzz, Jocko, Curly, Pogo and Doc all wanted to be in the coconut tree, but only the first three up could stay.

2. Fuzz went up before Curly and after Doc.

3. Pogo went up after Curly.

4. Jocko went up after Doc and before Fuzz.

5. Who got to stay in the tree?

STEP 2
Following a Format

The Short Report

We read and hear short reports every day—stories in the newspaper, reports on the radio, summaries of baseball games and reports of meetings. Each kind of report requires that the writer answer the same three questions that you learned in the last unit—Who am I? Who is my reader? What do I want to say?

Short reports, as well as longer ones, must present all of the necessary facts and must put them together in an order that makes sense. Some of the common ways to organize facts are to put them in **time order**, **in order of importance** or in **alphabetical order**.

Certain kinds of reports require specific information. These reports (such as book reports) are usually set up in a special **format**. That means that nearly every report of that type will follow the same pattern of presenting information.

The formats not only help to present the information; they also help us to remember to include all of the facts.

36

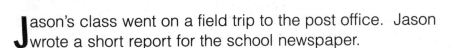

Reporting a Group Activity

Jason's class went on a field trip to the post office. Jason wrote a short report for the school newspaper.

Mrs. Helmsley's sixth grade class visited the post office on Tuesday, November 8th. Mr. Alvin Gunther, who is Gary Gunther's father, led the tour.

First, the students visited the mailroom, where they saw the mail being collected and sorted. Then, they learned about packages and how they are separated into classes according to weight and size. Last, the students visited the customer service center, and each student received a free booklet for collecting stamps.

When the class members returned to school, each student wrote a thank-you note to Mr. Gunther.

The Format

1. Notice that the first sentence of the report told **who**, **what**, **where** and **when**. Most short reports for newspapers are written this way.

2. The second paragraph told what happened in **time order**. Every kind of report needs to be presented in a logical order that readers can understand easily.

3. The final paragraph is a **conclusion**. It tells what the students did to respond to Mr. Gunther's kindness.

Think of something that you have done with a group, and write a report of the activity. You may want to use something that you and your family have done together.

Book reports are a way for us to share what we have read with other people. Good reports not only tell a little about what is in the book, but they also include an **opinion** of the reader. (An opinion is a statement of how you feel about something.) The opinion should be backed up by facts that support your feelings.

The format for a book report usually includes the following:

> Name of the book
> Author's name
> Type of book (fiction or nonfiction)
> Purpose of the book (to entertain or to inform)
> Summary of the book
>> Introduction (What the book is about)
>> Overall view of the story (one short paragraph)
>> One or two specific incidents from the story
> General comment and opinion (Was the book too long or too short? Did you like the book? Why or why not?)

An example of a book report appears on the following page. Notice that the main portion of the report is the summary and that the overall view of the story is written using **time order**.

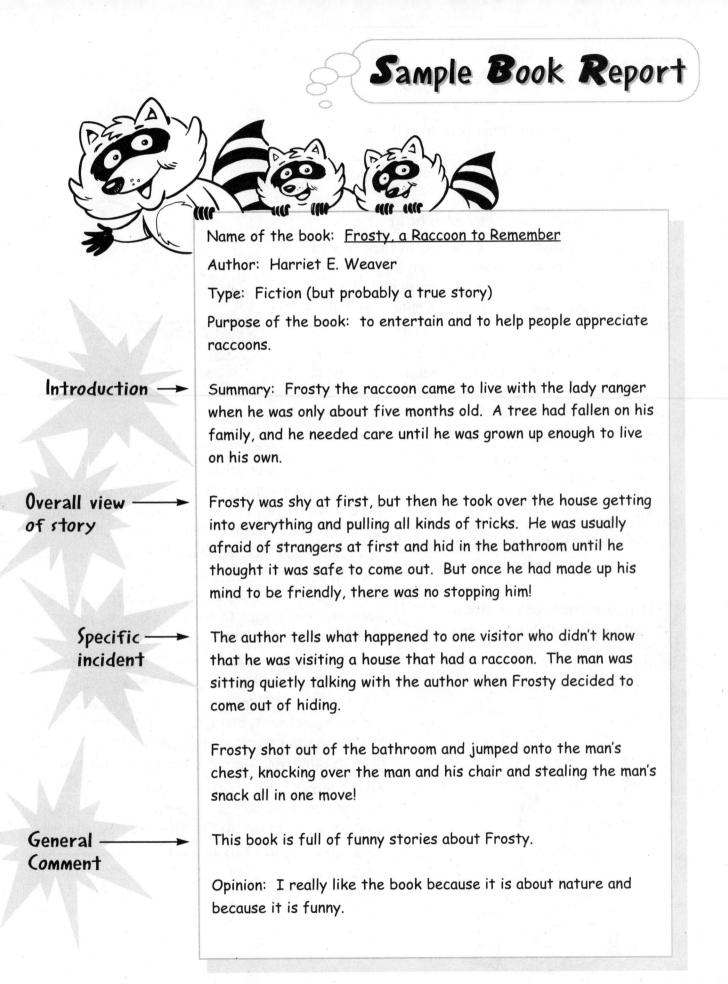

Name of the book: <u>Frosty, a Raccoon to Remember</u>

Author: Harriet E. Weaver

Type: Fiction (but probably a true story)

Purpose of the book: to entertain and to help people appreciate raccoons.

Introduction →

Summary: Frosty the raccoon came to live with the lady ranger when he was only about five months old. A tree had fallen on his family, and he needed care until he was grown up enough to live on his own.

Overall view of story →

Frosty was shy at first, but then he took over the house getting into everything and pulling all kinds of tricks. He was usually afraid of strangers at first and hid in the bathroom until he thought it was safe to come out. But once he had made up his mind to be friendly, there was no stopping him!

Specific incident →

The author tells what happened to one visitor who didn't know that he was visiting a house that had a raccoon. The man was sitting quietly talking with the author when Frosty decided to come out of hiding.

Frosty shot out of the bathroom and jumped onto the man's chest, knocking over the man and his chair and stealing the man's snack all in one move!

General Comment →

This book is full of funny stories about Frosty.

Opinion: I really like the book because it is about nature and because it is funny.

Writing a Summary

To summarize a story means to give the overall picture of the story in a few sentences. Read the story below, and choose the best summary.

One Saturday Morning

Anna and her father were in the car on their way to the grocery store when, suddenly, her father slammed on the brakes. The car screeched to a stop near a small blue basket in the middle of the street.

"There's a baby in that basket!" cried Anna's father, and he jumped out of the car and ran to the basket. At the sound of the screeching brakes, several people gathered around, and they came up to see what was in the basket, too.

"Why would anybody leave a baby in the street? Whose can it be?" people asked.

Anna's father decided that he should take the baby to the police station. He picked up the basket and started toward the car.

Just then a small red car with out-of-state license plates came roaring up and stopped.

A young woman was driving, and two small children were in the back seat. The woman got out and ran toward Anna's father and the basket. "Sir, that's my baby!" she screamed. "Please, is he all right?"

She pulled back the cover on the baby and studied the tiny body. "Oh, my sweet one, are you all right?" she asked. She looked at him quietly for a little while and then began to smile. "I believe you're just fine thanks to this kind man."

Then she turned to Anna's father and explained, "I put the baby's basket on the ground while I was getting the other children into the car. We were late for an appointment, and I forgot that little Davey was still on the trunk. I'm so grateful that he's not hurt and that you saw him before a car hit him."

Anna's father helped the woman put the baby into her car and buckle his basket securely. The other two children began to talk to the baby and play with him.

Then Anna and her father went on to the grocery store.

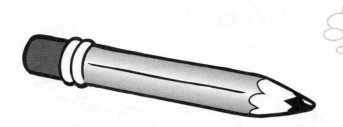

Writing a Summary

Circle the number of the selection that best summarizes the story. Then tell what is missing in each of the other selections.

1. Anna and her father were on their way to the grocery store, but they had to stop. After a while, they got to go to the store.

2. A baby was left in the street. Anna's father saw the baby and stopped his car. He took care of the baby until the mother realized what had happened and came back for the child.

3. A woman was anxious to get to an appointment, and she forgot her baby.

_____

_____

_____

_____

Writing an Opinion

Tell whether or not you liked the story you just read. Why or why not?

_____

_____

_____

_____

Practice Writing a Book Report

Choose a book that you have read recently, and write a report on it in the same form as on page 39. Be sure to include your opinion of the book.

_____

_____

_____

_____

_____

_____

_____

_____

_____

_____

_____

_____

_____

_____

Do you ever watch a news report on television?

Who is the audience? (You and other viewers.)

What is the relationship of the newscaster to the audience? (The newscaster is performing a service for the audience.)

What does he or she want to say? (The newscaster wants to give the facts of the stories that he or she thinks are important.)

A news story includes all of the most important facts in the first paragraph of the story.

The Five Basic Points

Who did the action?
What did they do?
Where did it happen?
When did it take place?
Why did the person or persons do it?

The following paragraphs add details going from the more important details to the less important ones. If a newspaper is short on space or a television program has very limited time, the story can be cut near the end without losing any important details.

Read the following example, and see if the story includes each of the five basic points.

Which
ones
are
missing?

Students Walk for Injured Fireman

Anytown—Sixth grade students at Fairview School held a walk-a-thon at the school to raise money for John Martinez, a fireman who lost the use of his legs earlier this year when a wall collapsed and fell on him. Martinez is the uncle of one of the students in the class.

The sixth graders collected more than $400 for the Martinez family by taking pledges and walking a total of 154 miles.

Practice Arranging Facts in Order

Facts for a news story should be arranged in order of importance with the most important facts first. Read all the facts for the stories below, and then number them in the correct order for a news story.

Example:

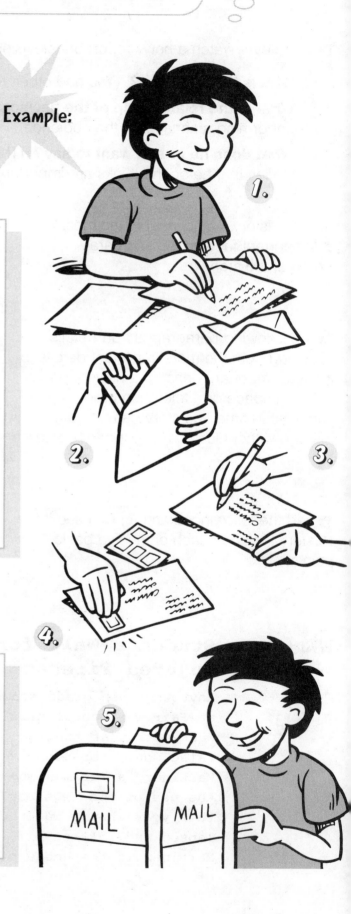

A. _____ No one was hurt in the collision.

_____ A car and a gasoline truck collided near Jefferson City Hall Thursday afternoon.

_____ The car was from Illinois.

_____ The car had rolled down the hill from a parking spot.

_____ The names of the drivers of the vehicles were not released.

B. _____ The new moon weighs approximately six tons.

_____ Scientists discovered a new moon on Jupiter.

_____ This is the first such discovery since 1800.

_____ The new moon has been named Harvest.

Is Anything Missing?

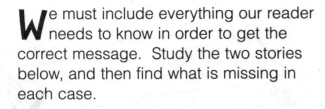

We must include everything our reader needs to know in order to get the correct message. Study the two stories below, and then find what is missing in each case.

Story 1

Mr. Leon Fairchild was awarded first prize at the county fair during Thursday's competition.

The prize, a 50-lb. sack of oats, was donated by the Farmers' Oat Co. in Clinton.

Fairchild says he will enter the state competition at Fairview in March.

What is missing?

_____

_____

_____

_____

What is missing?

_____

_____

_____

_____

_____

Story 2

The accident happened at the intersection of Main and Grandview at 2:00 p.m. on Monday.

Police report no injuries, but damages were estimated at $2000.

Name_____

Writing a News Report

Write a short report (true or made up) of a news happening. You may use a historical incident if you like. Be certain that the first paragraph includes the answers to the questions "who, what, when, where and why." Leave a blank space at the top of your story for a headline, which you will add later.

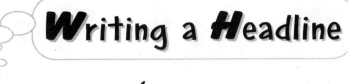

Writing a Headline

If you look at a newspaper, you will see many headlines. Most of them give an idea of what the story below is about, but some are written just to draw your attention.

A good headline is short. It contains an action word or implies one. It tells something about the story and attracts the reader to read it.

Example: Two-Year-Old Saves Mother

Example: Bay City Eagles Fly over Sarasota (sports story)

Try writing a short headline for each of the examples below. When you have finished, go back and place a headline on the news story you wrote earlier.

1.   A 13-year-old boy wants to try for a pilot's license.

_____

2.   The remains of a 65-million-year-old dinosaur were discovered in Colorado near Denver.

_____

3.   A world-famous concert musician has just purchased a fast-food chicken business.

_____

Reporting to a Group

If you belong to a youth group or school organization, you may be asked to get information for the group. The report below shows how John presented information that he had collected about t-shirts. Notice the three parts of his report.

1. **Where did you get the information?**

2. **What is the information?**

3. **Recommendation**

T-Shirt Research

I called two places about the cost of t-shirts for our class. Stars and Bars would sell us all-cotton t-shirts for $5.00 apiece. Big Barn would sell us cotton and polyester t-shirts at $4.75 each.

I would recommend that we buy from Big Barn because cotton and polyester will not shrink as easily as plain cotton and because Big Barn's t-shirts are less expensive.

By John Johnson

Name_____

Suppose that you belong to a class or a group that has talked about going on a field trip to see some places in the city. You did research and found the following information. Write a short report on what you found, and include a recommendation about what the group should do for a field trip.

A bus tour of the city costs $15 per person.

Admission to the zoo is $3.00.

Admission to the museum is $5.00.

Theater tickets are $6.00.

_____

_____

_____

_____

_____

_____

_____

_____

_____

_____

_____

Name _____

Use the words on the right to complete the sentences below.

action

author

opinion

first

summary

missing

most

1. The _____ is a short overview of the whole book.

2. When you state whether or not you like the book, you are giving your _____.

3. The name of the person who wrote the book is the _____.

4. A news report has the _____ important news first.

5. The _____ paragraph of a news report should tell who, what, where, when and why.

6. The headline of a news article includes an _____ word or implies one.

7. News articles must be checked to be certain that no information is _____.

50

Just for Fun

See if you can think of something that each of these terms might be describing. Then try creating your own descriptive terms.

1. pear-shaped

_____

2. terrifying

_____

3. slimy green

_____

4. pale pink

_____

5. wrinkled

_____

_____

_____

_____

_____

STEP 3
Writing a Formal Report

Gathering Information

A formal report is usually longer than the reports that you did in the last section, and most of the time a formal report includes information from several sources. Information can come from books, encyclopedias, interviews, speeches, personal experiences, etc.

Brad was on vacation in Alabama when he saw an armadillo. Later, after Brad returned home, he decided to read more about armadillos in order to give a report to his scout group.

These are the steps that Brad followed in gathering information for his report:

1. Brad thought about the three basic questions–"Who am I? Who is my reader? What do I want to say?" Brad decided that the other members of the group would probably be interested in the same things that interested him.

2. He decided to look in the library for information about armadillos.

3. First, Brad read an article about armadillos in an encyclopedia. He recorded the name and volume number of the encyclopedia and the page number of the article. The encyclopedia article provided Brad with clues about other places to look.

4. Next, Brad used the library index system to look for books on armadillos. He used the word *animal* to find books that describe animals. When he saw books listed that he thought would have something about armadillos, he went to the shelves and looked at many books in the same area.

5. Brad looked up the word *armadillo* in the index of each book that interested him. When he found several books that mentioned armadillos, he checked them out and took them home to read.

Brad gathered more information than he could use. He knew that he would have to decide how much of it would work well in his report. How did he make his decision?

1. First, Brad thought about what he read that interested him the most, and he wrote down his thoughts. Brad felt that whatever interested him would probably interest his friends, too. Here is what Brad wrote.

The armadillo looks like a pig. Sometimes it acts like one, too.
It has a shell like a turtle. The shell protects the animal from enemies.
The armadillo eats like an anteater. It sleeps underground.
It walks underwater. It hides from enemies by curling up into a ball.

2. Then Brad grouped these thoughts in much the same way as you grouped thoughts from brainstorming on page 10.

The armadillo looks like a combination of three different animals.
    It is the size of a pig.
    It has a shell like a turtle.
    It eats like an anteater.
The armadillo has a strange life-style.
    It sleeps underground.
    It walks underwater.
    It hides from its enemies by curling up into a ball.

Brad's work helped him to write an **outline**. (See next page.) Notice how he used Roman numerals to label the main ideas and capital letters to label the lesser ideas. If he had included other ideas under each capital letter, he would have used small numerals to label them.

Building an Outline

Brad decided to write an **outline** before writing his report so that all of his thoughts would be in a logical order. The outline had five parts—the **title**, the **opening statement**, the **thesis sentence**, the **body** (the largest part of the outline) and the **list of sources** (bibliography).

Title: The World's Strangest Animal

Opening Statement: Can you imagine an animal that is a combination of a pig, a turtle and an anteater?

Thesis Sentence: An armadillo is a strange animal both in looks and in life-style.

Body:
    I. The armadillo looks like three different animals.
        A. It is the size of a pig.
        B. It has a shell like a turtle.
        C. Its tongue and front legs and claws are like those of an anteater.

    II. The armadillo has a strange life-style.
        A. It sleeps underground.
        B. It eats insects and worms.
        C. It hides from enemies by curling up into a ball.
        D. It walks underwater instead of swimming.

    III. Conclusion: Don't you agree that the armadillo is "The World's Strangest Animal"?

Sources: Encyclopedia Americana. Vol. 2, 1993, p. 328.

Limburg, Peter. What's in the Names of Wild Animals? Coward, McCann & Geoghegan, 1977, pp. 23-34.

Zappler, Lisbeth, Nature's Oddballs. Doubleday and Company, Inc., Garden City, New York, 1978, pp. 105-106.

Building an Outline

Brad used his outline as a guide to writing his report and added information under each topic heading as it made sense. He found that he could not use all of the information that he had because some of it did not fit anywhere on the outline.

After Brad had written his report, he proofread his paper. You will find pages on proofreading later in this section and a checklist that you can use for your work.

The World's Strangest Animal

by Brad Brown

Can you imagine an animal that is a combination of a pig, a turtle and an anteater? That is an armadillo. An armadillo's looks and its life-style are both very strange.

The armadillo looks like three different animals–a pig, a turtle and an anteater. It is about the size of a pig, but an armadillo has a hard shell, and a pig does not.

The armadillo is like a turtle because both of them have shells outside their bodies. However, the turtle shell is in one piece, and the armadillo shell has several movable pieces. Some armadillos also have hair between the shell plates, but turtles do not have hair.

An armadillo is like an anteater because both anteaters and armadillos have strong legs with sharp claws. Armadillos also have long, sticky tongues like anteaters do.

An armadillo not only looks strange, it has a strange life-style, too. It sleeps under the ground in a burrow during the day and comes out in the evening to eat. It eats plants, insects and worms–ugh!

Building an Outline

Brad Brown–The World's Strangest Animal

p. 2

Armadillos are timid animals, and they are most afraid of coyotes. If an armadillo sees a coyote, the armadillo will either bury itself as fast as it can or will roll into a ball with its shell plates on the outside. It hopes that the coyote will not be able to break into the shell with its sharp teeth.

> "There is a report of an armadillo observed digging its way into earth so hard a person would need a pickax to penetrate. It had buried itself completely in just two minutes." (Zappler)

Another unusual thing about armadillos is the way they cross water. Their bodies are so heavy that they cannot swim, so when an armadillo must cross a creek or lake, it usually walks across the bottom. If the trip is too far to walk, the armadillo swallows a lot of air so that it is able to float across the water.

Now you can see why an armadillo is a combination of a pig, a turtle and an anteater. It needs qualities from all three animals in order to survive its very strange life-style. Do you agree with me that the armadillo is "The World's Strangest Animal"?

Sources:

Encyclopedia Americana. Vol. 2, 1993, p. 328.

Limburg, Peter. What's in the Names of Wild Animals? Coward, McCann & Geoghegan, 1977, pp. 23-34.

Zappler, Lisbeth, Nature's Oddballs. Doubleday and Company, Inc., Garden City, New York, 1978, pp. 105-106.

Name _____

Writing a Grabber Title

The title of any work is the first thing that attracts the reader's eye. A "grabber" title can make the difference between having someone read what you have written or push it aside. Writing a title is easier when you know a few tricks to catch the reader's attention.

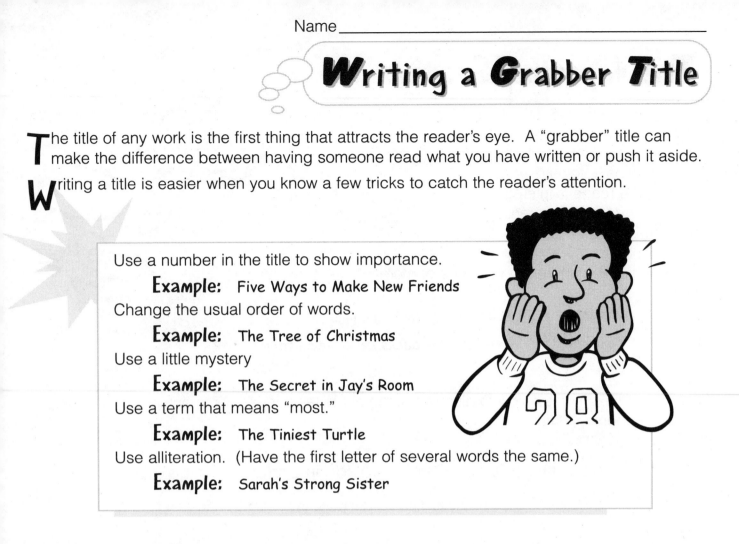

Use a number in the title to show importance.

Example: Five Ways to Make New Friends

Change the usual order of words.

Example: The Tree of Christmas

Use a little mystery

Example: The Secret in Jay's Room

Use a term that means "most."

Example: The Tiniest Turtle

Use alliteration. (Have the first letter of several words the same.)

Example: Sarah's Strong Sister

Try your luck at perking up the following titles by using the tricks above:

1. A little boy's small clock

   _____

2. A story about people searching for gold in the mountains

   _____

3. Jill's new jumping exercises

   _____

4. The kangaroo that hid its baby

   _____

5. Finding something you like to do

   _____

57

The Opening Statement

How will you attract your reader and interest him in what you have to say? A large part of the reader's interest depends upon your opening statement.

Which statement below would be of more interest to you?

Example 1: Ducks are interesting animals.

Example 2: Why is it that ducks never seem to get lost?

Study the examples below to discover some of the techniques commonly used for writing good opening statements.

1. Use a **specific number** to provide important startling information.

   Example: Over half a million people were affected by the flood.

2. Mention **money**.

   Example: You can make $100 in 15 minutes.

3. Begin with a **question**.

   Example: Do you know of an animal that can run 50 miles an hour?

4. Mention a **universal interest** such as making friends or feeling secure.

   Example: Have you ever been at a party where you had to stand around and wait for someone to talk to?

Be certain that your opening statement is directly connected with your topic. If it is not, you may lose your reader's attention before he or she ever gets started.

Practice with Opening Statements

Each of the following exercises lists two possibilities for an opening statement. Circle the statement that would interest you as a reader.

1. a. Did you ever see a footprint that was six feet long?

    b. This paper is about dinosaurs.

2. a. The Mississippi River flooded many people's homes.

    b. Have you ever had to stay overnight with 400 other people in a shelter?

3. a. John Brown helped the slaves escape.

    b. A secret Underground Railroad played an important part in our nation's history.

4. a. You can make $200 a month in your spare time.

    b. Baby-sitting is a good part-time job.

5. a. Skating is good exercise.

    b. You can meet new friends, hear great music and get your exercise for only about $4.00!

How could the following opening statements be made more interesting? Rewrite them using the suggestions on the previous page.

1. My paper is about cats.

    _____

2. A lot of things go on in an anthill.

    _____

3. My favorite food is bananas.

    _____

4. Trash is a national problem.

    _____

5. I like to watch football games.

    _____

Writing the Thesis Sentence

The thesis sentence helps the reader to organize his thoughts so that he will understand the information he is about to receive. A thesis sentence is like a topic sentence except that it introduces an essay rather than a paragraph.

Usually, the thesis sentence has two parts–the **topic** and a mention of each of the **main points** you plan to cover about that topic. Study the following examples to see how a thesis sentence is written.

Example 1

Thesis Sentence: We need water for everyday living–for drinking and bathing, for growing food and for recreation and transportation.

Main Points of Essay:
I. We need water for drinking and bathing.
II. We need water for growing food.
III. We need water for recreation and transportation.

Example 2

Thesis Sentence: Knowing a foreign language can help you to build your vocabulary, to learn how other people live and to make friends with people from other countries.

Main Points of Essay:
I. Knowing a foreign language can help you to build your vocabulary.
II. Knowing a foreign language can help you to learn how other people live.
III. Knowing a foreign language can help you to make friends with people from other countries.

Practice Writing Thesis Sentences

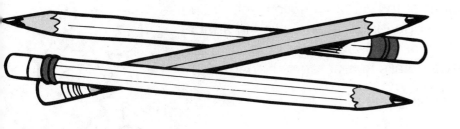

Write a thesis sentence for each of the following groups of main ideas.

1. _____

Some people ride the ferry to work every morning.

Many people travel to work by train.

Most people drive their cars to work.

2. _____

Mountain rescue teams use dogs to locate survivors in the snow.

Fire fighters use dogs to detect smoke.

Police officers use dogs to detect illegal drugs.

3. _____

Weavers display their artistic abilities in the blankets they make.

Automobile painters often add colorful murals to the bodies of cars.

Chain saw sculptors show their work in roadside galleries.

4. _____

Most people watch at least one news program on TV every day.

At least half of the population subscribes to a daily newspaper.

Some people get their news on-line.

5. _____

Many Italian foods are made using wheat pasta.

Several Mexican foods are made using corn products.

German people often use rye flour in their foods.

Arranging Topics in an Outline

When you write, you want your reader to be able to follow your thoughts without getting lost. You can arrange topics in an outline in **spatial order, time order, least-to-most** or **most-to-least order** in much the same way as you learned to arrange details in a paragraph (page 19).

You may also want to think about using one of the following methods:

1. Step-by-Step Order

Thesis Sentence Example: Training a dog to obey requires several steps—developing trust, teaching the dog to come and then teaching more difficult commands.

2. Order of Importance

Notice that the thesis sentence here is actually more than one sentence.

Thesis Sentence Example: When a person has had an accident, first you check his or her breathing. Next, you stop any bleeding. Finally, pay attention to other parts of the body.

Decide which order would probably be the best selection for each of the topics below.

1. A report that describes several stops that Lewis and Clark made as they traveled along the Mississippi River

_____

2. A description of how to build a raft

_____

3. Directions on planning a large party

_____

4. A guide for learning how to manage money

_____

5. An essay on how to appreciate rap music

_____

62

Listing Sources (Making a Bibliography)

Whenever you use someone else's material in your work, you should give them credit for their part in it. We use a list of sources (also called a **bibliography**) at the end of a report to include all those books, speeches, etc., that went into making our paper.

If you have used a short quote from someone's exact words, place quotation marks around the material. Then give credit by placing the last name of the author in parentheses following the quote. At the end of the paper, mention the full source.

Example: "Four score and seven years ago our fathers brought forth on this continent, a new nation, conceived in Liberty, and dedicated to the proposition that all men are created equal." (Lincoln)

At the End of the Paper:

Lincoln, Abraham. Speech at Gettysburg, Pennsylvania, November 19, 1863.

The list of sources should be written in **alphabetical order, author's name first**. The following examples will help you to set up each kind of source.

Books

Jones, Arthur. <u>Learning from the Sun</u>. January Press, 1994, p. 36.

Magazine Article

Jones, Arthur. "Sunspots and Human Behavior," <u>National Scientist</u>. Vol. III, 1994, pp. 2-4.

Encyclopedia

<u>Encyclopedia Americana</u>. Vol. 4, 1993, pp. 4-7.

Speech

Martin, Marvin. "The Sun in Your Eyes," Speech at Viva State University, May 8, 1994.

Note: Other formats for biographical entries may be required for some publications.

Name_____

Practice Writing a Bibliography

Write the following sources in correct bibliographical form.
Then decide which would come first, second, third, etc.

1. Author: Stephen Crane
   Book: *The Red Badge of Courage*
   Publisher: Pocket Books, Inc.
   Date: 1954
   Page: 37

   _____

   _____

2. Author: Jill Smolowe
   Article: "Shadow Play"
   Magazine: *Time*
   Dates: May 23, 1994
   Pages: 32-34

   _____

   _____

3. Author: Martin Luther King
   Speech in Washington, D.C.
   Date: August 28, 1963

   _____

   _____

The Finishing Touch—Proofreading

Proofreading for Content

Remember that the most important part of writing is to get your message across to the reader. Check these steps, and see how well you have done!

1. Do you have an eye-catching title?

2. Does the first paragraph grab the reader's attention and include the thesis sentence?

3. Read your work aloud to others. Do they understand what you were saying? Do you need to correct punctuation or arrange word groups differently?

4. Do you have a sentence or paragraph that ends the work and lets the reader know what you would like for him or her to think or to do? (Informative pieces do not need this kind of ending.) Remember that a good conclusion often refers back to the opening statement.

Name_____

Proofreading for Mechanics–Capitalization

For each rule listed below, write a sentence that illustrates the rule.

1. Capitalize the first letter of every sentence.

_____

_____

2. Always capitalize the word "I."

_____

_____

3. Capitalize important words in titles.

_____

_____

4. Capitalize names and holidays.

_____

_____

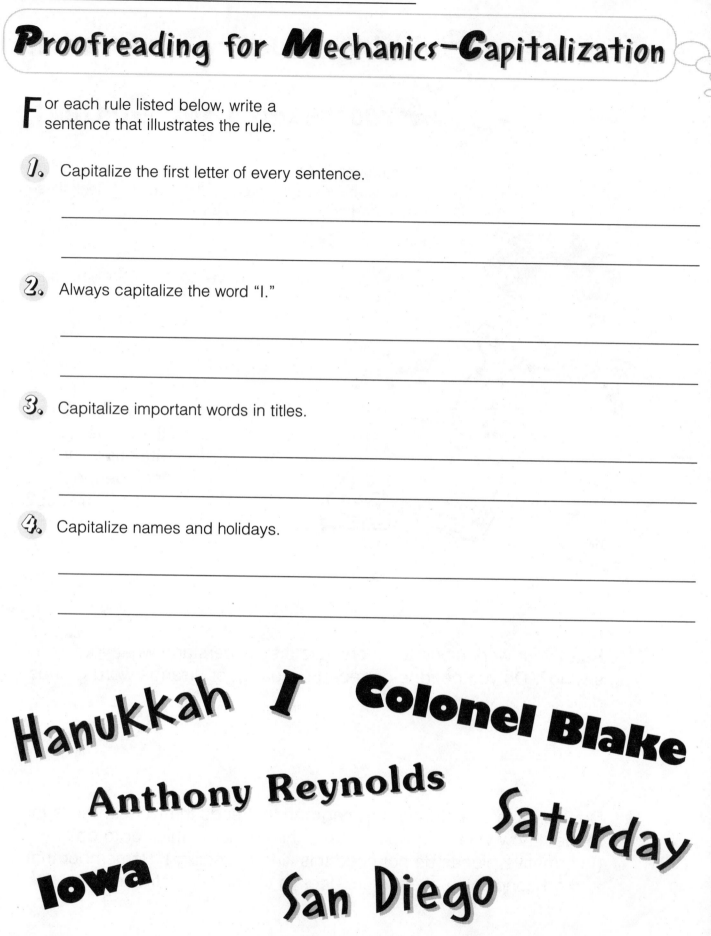

Hanukkah   I   Colonel Blake

Anthony Reynolds

Saturday

Iowa   San Diego

Proofreading for Mechanics-Punctuation

By now you have been using correct punctuation for most occasions. The following exercise is to remind you of any general rules that you may have forgotten. Write an example to illustrate each rule.

1. Use a period after a statement.

_____

2. Use a question mark at the end of a question.

_____

3. Use an exclamation mark after a sentence that shows strong feeling.

_____

4. Use a comma to separate words in a series such as one, two, three.

_____

5. Use a comma to separate the city and the state in an address.

_____

6. Use a comma after an introductory phrase. (Example: After swimming, Amy went to the library.)

_____

7. Use commas to set off words that interrupt the flow of the sentence. (Example: Amos, the oldest, voted to go to the movies.)

_____

8. Use quotation marks to set off the words someone actually said.

_____

Name_____

Checklist for Proofreading

Content

Eye-catching title

Statement of purpose

Good flow of thought

Satisfactory end

Reads Well Aloud

Mechanics–Punctuation

Appropriate end marks

Commas used in series, dates, addresses

Comma after an introductory phrase

Comma to set off words that interrupt the flow of the sentence

Comma before conjunction in a compound sentence (See page 84.)

Comma after first thought in a sentence beginning with a subordinating conjunction (See page 86.)

Quotation marks and direct quotes

Mechanics–Capitalization

First letter of every sentence

All names and the word "I"

Titles

Holidays

Sentence Structure

No fragments

No run-on sentences

Variety of structures

Subject-verb agreement

Pronoun-noun agreement

Modifiers placed correctly

Active rather than passive verbs most of the time (See page 76.)

Writing Your Own Formal Report

Choose a topic that interests you, and gather the information you need. Then follow the guide below to develop your own outline and formal report.

Title: _____

Opening Statement: _____

_____

_____

Thesis Sentence: _____

_____

_____

Body: _____

_____

_____

_____

_____

_____

_____

_____

Sources: _____

_____

_____

Remember to proofread your work!

Name _____

1. The title of any work is the first thing that a reader notices. Circle the better title below.

> My Little Elephant
>
> Rajah and the Rainbow Bird

2. The opening statement grabs the reader's attention and prepares him for what will follow. Which of the following statements is a better choice for an opening statement?

> There are a lot of elephants in India.
>
> Some people in India say that elephants are smarter than people.

3. The thesis sentence gives an overview of the report and prepares the reader for what to expect. It presents topics in the order in which they will appear in the report. What topics would you expect to follow this thesis sentence?

> The Indian elephant is honored for several reasons–its brave spirit, its unusual intelligence and its exceptional strength.

_____

_____

_____

4. A bibliography is written in alphabetical order according to the author's _____ name.

70

Mark used the letters of his name to write words that described his personality.

M ⊸ marvelous, muscular

A ⊸ athletic

R ⊸ runner

K ⊸ kind

Now it's your turn.

_____
_____
_____
_____
_____
_____
_____
_____

STEP 4
Making Your Writing Sparkle

Part 1: Using Specific Nouns, Descriptive Verbs and Active Voice

Specific Nouns

Now you are at the point as a writer where you can start to "fine tune" your work. You can look for ways to make what you want to say more interesting and more powerful.

One of the tricks of professional writers is to use **specific nouns** rather than general nouns and pronouns.

Example

General: The man hid behind a barrel.

Specific: Mr. August hid behind a barrel.

By using specific nouns in place of general ones, we make writing come alive for the reader. Let's look at another example.

Example

General: The animal lifted its head and made a sound.

Specific: The buffalo lifted her head and moaned.

Name_____

Rewrite each of the following sentences, changing general nouns and pronouns to specific ones where you can.

1. The little girl looked at the building.

_____

2. A bird hovered over the child.

_____

3. We fed it.

_____

4. We watched it fly away.

_____

5. She waved to it.

_____

As you know, verbs are the "doors" of the sentence. The more action and life in the verb, the better your writing will be.

Look at the following examples:

Examples: The boy **walked** toward the playground.

Manuel **skipped** toward the playground.

Greg **strolled** toward the playground.

Joseph **bounded** toward the playground.

The verb *walked* could be replaced by the verbs *skipped*, *strolled* or *bounded*. Can you think of other words that could replace *walked*?

Verbs that really show what is happening are called **descriptive verbs**. Study the following examples to see what verbs can be used to replace *looked*.

Examples: Sharon **looked** at the tablecloth.

Sharon **stared** at the tablecloth.

Sharon **peeked** at the tablecloth.

Both *stared* and *peeked* give the reader a better picture than *looked*.

Caution: Do not replace every verb with a descriptive verb, or your writing will appear to be insincere.

Practice Using Descriptive Verbs

Rewrite the following paragraph using specific nouns and descriptive verbs.

The boy liked to fish in the river. He walked to the curve in the river and cast in his line. The fish bit at the bait. The boy caught the fish. Then he walked home with it.

_____

_____

_____

_____

_____

_____

_____

_____

_____

_____

_____

Name_____

Active and Passive Voice

Study the following examples, and decide which is more interesting:

Examples

Active: The turtle ate the bug.

Passive: The bug was eaten by the turtle.

Verbs in a sentence are stronger and more interesting if they are in active voice. *Active voice* means that the subject (in this case "turtle") is doing the acting as in "The turtle ate the bug." Notice that in the example for passive voice, the bug is the subject, and it is being acted upon. Try to keep most of your writing in active, rather than passive, voice.

Examples

Active: The truck ran over the wagon.

Passive: The wagon was run over by the truck.

Change the passive voice to active in each of the following sentences:

1. John was helped by the fire fighter.

   _____

2. The dog was chased by the police officer.

   _____

3. The apple was eaten by me.

   _____

4. The letter was sent by Susan.

   _____

5. The thief was caught by the police officer.

   _____

6. The fire was built by the old woodcutter.

   _____

Name_____

Think about something you have done that you enjoyed remembering, and write a paragraph or two about it. When you have finished, look over your work to see if you have used any of the things you have learned in this section.

Enclose your paragraph in a letter for a friend or family member to enjoy.

Name_____

Part 2: Using Modifiers to Add Color

Adjectives

Adjectives are words that tell us something about the noun. They answer the questions "What kind?" "How many?" or "Which one?"

We can use adjectives to make our writing more interesting and more colorful.

Example 1

Basic Sentence: The man bought a ticket to Grand Rapids.

Adding Adjectives: The **short**, **bald** man bought a **one-way** ticket to Grand Rapids.

Example 2

Basic Sentence: A house with a porch stood before him.

Adding Adjectives: A **shabby little** house with a **green** porch stood before him.

Add colorful adjectives to the following nouns:

1. _____ pencil

2. _____ ball

3. _____ truck

4. _____ child

5. _____ woman

6. _____ store

7. _____ boat

8. _____ sweater

9. _____ football

78

Prepositional Phrases Used as Adjectives

Prepositional phrases can act as adjectives. When they do, they tell "what kind," "how many" or "which one."

Example 1: Gail's friend came to the musical.

Gail's friend **from Hollywood** came to the musical **at our school**.

Example 2: The lights came crashing down.

The lights **above Ted** came crashing down.

Add a prepositional phrase to each of the following nouns:

Example: the man <u>in the story</u>

Common Prepositions
under
over
between
beside
near
to
of
for
from
along
in
after
at

1. the little girl _____

2. a tiny mouse _____

3. a ball of yarn _____

4. several small children _____

5. a funny old lamp _____

Name_____

Practice Using Adjectives and Prepositional Phrases

Write a short description of the picture below. Use at least two colorful adjectives and/or prepositional phrases in your description.

Adverbs

Adverbs describe a verb, another adverb or an adjective They answer the questions "Where?" "When?" "How?" and "To what extent?" Many adverbs end in *ly.*

Example 1: This piece of the puzzle goes *there*!
There explains where the piece goes.

Example 2: I went to the mall *yesterday.*
Yesterday tells when I went.

Example 3: Carrie smiled *shyly.*
Shyly explains how Carrie smiled.

Example 4: Gilbert was *completely* lost.
Completely explains to what extent Gilbert was lost.

Choose adverbs from the list below that help describe the verbs, adverbs or adjectives in the following exercise.

Adverbs

here
now
boldly
silently
quickly
tomorrow
later
grimly
eagerly
there
very

1. Put the package _____, please.

2. The postman will come _____.

3. She ran _____ to the door.

4. He stood _____ beside the police car.

5. We cannot let her come _____.

6. _____ we will light the candles.

7. _____ get ready to hear the story.

8. Camilla slipped _____ out of her room.

9. Who could be _____ waiting?

Prepositional Phrases Used as Adverbs

You already know that prepositional phrases can be used as adjectives to describe nouns. They can also be used as adverbs to describe verbs, adverbs or adjectives.

Prepositional phrases that tell where, when, how or to what extent are being used as adverbs.

WHERE?
WHEN?
HOW?

Example 1: Aaron peeked *under the pillow.*

Under the pillow tells where Aaron peeked.

Example 2: *After the game,* we went to the ice cream store.

After the game tells when we went.

Example 3: John worked *like a beaver* to finish his project.

Like a beaver tells how John worked. (We often say someone is "as busy as a beaver.")

Example 4: Lucia sank *to her waist* in the mud.

To her waist tells to what extent she sank. *In the mud* is also a prepositional phrase used as an adverb. It tells where she sank.

Underline the adverbial prepositional phrase in each sentence below. Then tell whether the phrase is being used to tell where, when, how or to what extent.

1. Liza sneaked into the kitchen. _____

2. She looked inside the refrigerator, but she found nothing interesting. _____

3. Then she searched the cabinet for several minutes. _____

4. She searched with great enthusiasm, but still she found nothing. _____

5. After her search, Liza went back to bed. (2) _____   _____

Name _____

Practice Using Adverbs and Prepositional Phrases

Write a short description of what is happening here. Use at least two adverbs or prepositional phrases used as adverbs.

_____

_____

_____

_____

_____

_____

_____

Name_____

Compound Sentences

Look at the following piece of writing:

> Jerry painted the house. I painted the garage. The day was hot. We worked hard. Jerry got tired. I did, too.

Too many short, choppy sentences in a row interrupt the reader's flow of thought. We can combine sentences to make the flow of words smoother by using **coordinating conjunctions**.

When we combine two complete thoughts by using one of the coordinating conjunctions, we always put a comma before the coordinating conjunction.

> **Example:** Jerry painted the house, *and* I painted the garage.

Common Coordinating Conjunctions
and
but
or
for
yet

Notice how the following two thoughts can be combined:

> **Example:** The dog needed to be brushed. I didn't want to brush him.
>
> The dog needed to be brushed, *but* I didn't want to brush him.

When we join two complete sentences together by using a comma and a coordinating conjunction, we form a **compound sentence**.

Circle the compound sentences in the following paragraph:

Joan came running into the house. She was holding a letter in her hand, and she was very excited. "Mom! Mom!" she cried. "I got a letter from Aunt Jo, and she wants me to spend the summer with her! We can swim, and we can go horseback riding every day. That will be great!"

Name _____

Practice Combining Sentences

Rewrite the following sentences, improving them by combining sentences with the conjunctions *and*, *but* and *or*.

1. Joseph held the donkey. He watched it eat.

_____

2. The donkey had a heavy load. He didn't seem to mind it.

_____

3. Joseph may keep the donkey. He may sell it.

_____

4. Joseph has a wagon for the donkey. The wagon needs to be fixed.

_____

5. The wagon is small. It can hold only one person.

_____

Complex Sentences

When we studied compound sentences, we used coordinating conjunctions to connect two sentences of equal importance together. Now we will see how to join two sentences together when one thought is less important than the other. We will use **subordinating conjunctions**.

The word *subordinating* means that one thought is subordinate to (less important than) the other. *Sub* means "under."

Example: Ann wanted to go to the game.
Ann wanted to see her friend Sue.

Ann wanted to go to the game *because* she wanted to see her friend Sue.

In this example, *because* connects the two ideas. Notice that the first part of the sentence makes sense without the second part, but the second part does not make sense without the first part. A subordinating conjunction makes the thought that follows it dependent upon the rest of the sentence.

Let's look at another example.

Example: The snow was falling. Raul continued to paint his car.

Although the snow was falling, Raul continued to paint his car.

In this example *although* connects the two sentences. Do you see any difference in how this sentence is punctuated?

When the subordinate thought begins the sentence, we put a comma after it before we go on to the rest of the sentence. When the subordinate thought ends the sentence, no comma is needed.

Subordinating Conjunctions

after
although
because
if
since
unless
when
while
which
that
who
(and many others)

Name _____

Find the subordinate thoughts in the following paragraphs and underline them.

Hint: Look for subordinating conjunctions.

When Barry came home from Jack's house, he was grinning from ear to ear. "Jack has a new pet," he said. "He let me hold it because he had to do his chores."

"What kind of pet is it?" asked Barry's mother.

"If I tell you, will you let me have one, too?" teased Barry.

"I don't know," answered his mother. "If you would like to tell me, I could think about it."

"Since you're willing to think about it, I'll tell you," said Barry. "It's a turtle."

Each of the sentences below ends with a subordinate thought. Rewrite the sentences so that the subordinate thought comes at the beginning. Remember to use commas where they are needed.

1. I missed dinner because I was late getting home.

   _____

2. We can start a fire in the fireplace after the game ends.

   _____

3. I could deliver newspapers if I had a new bicycle.

   _____

Practice Writing Complex Sentences

When the subordinate thought begins the
sentence, we put a comma after it before
we go on to the rest of the sentence. When
the subordinate thought ends the sentence,
no comma is needed.

Rewrite the sentences below. Use the subordinating conjunctions if, *unless*, *since*,
because, *where* or *when* to form complex
sentences.

1. Jack hid behind the stack of hay. No one would find him.

_____

_____

2. He heard someone coming. He crouched down low.

_____

_____

3. The hay tickled Jack's nose. He sneezed.

_____

_____

4. The sheriff walked into the barn. He heard Jack sneeze.

_____

_____

5. The sheriff laughed. Jack came out of his hiding place.

_____

_____

HA!
HA!
Hee!
Hee!

Practice Using Compound and Complex Sentences

Most people enjoy telling anecdotes. An anecdote is a short story of someone's experience that is interesting or amusing. Write an anecdote describing an experience that you have had or someone you know has had. Use at least one coordinating conjunction and one subordinating conjunction in your story. Be sure to punctuate correctly.

Transitions

A reader can become confused when the writer moves from one thought to another. Good writers use **transitional words** to help the reader follow the train of thought.

Transitional Words

first, second, etc.
therefore
next
last
finally
thus
soon
now
(and many others)

1. We can direct the reader to a **change in time** by using words such as *now*, *soon*, *then*, *next*, *later* and *finally*.

Example: The warm sun began to melt the old winter snow. *Soon*, green grass and spring flowers appeared.

2. We can use words such as *therefore*, *thus*, *in addition to* and *unless* to **build a relationship** between what has already been said and what is about to follow.

Example: Erica had completed the assignment. *Therefore*, she deserved the grade she got.

3. Sometimes we can make the transition from one thought to another (or one paragraph to another) smoother by **repeating a key word** or a form of it.

Example: The snow fell daily until it reached a depth of nearly 30 inches. Each morning I plodded my way to the mailbox, but even the mailman with his Jeep had not been able to get through the deep snow. We felt alone and *isolated*.

Isolation was not our biggest problem, however . . .

Notice that the word *isolated* in the first paragraph is changed in form to *isolation* in the second paragraph. The repetition of the word keeps the flow of thought in the reader's mind.

Name_____

Practice with Transitions

Circle the transitional devices used in each of the following selections:

1. A small pig was stuck under a fallen log. Anna grasped the pig by its back legs and pulled and pulled, but the pig did not come free of the log.

   Then Anna used a sharp stick to dig dirt away from the log. The pig began to back out.

   Finally, Anna gave the pig one really hard tug, and it was free!

2. We watched the sunset until all that was left were a few pink rays above the mountains. The air was cool, and the night insects began to sing. It was a time of quiet peace . . .

   Peace didn't last long, however . . .

3. Jose sang in the school choir. He liked being with his friends, and he liked Mr. Jones, the choir director. He even liked wearing the big blue choir robe.

   Although Jose enjoyed being in the choir, his real love was rap music.

4. Winter sneaked in on us last year. Its soft whiteness just appeared one morning somewhere between raking the fall leaves and getting ready for the spring planting. And it was cold, very cold, but also very beautiful.

   The cold that came with winter was unwelcome.

5. Dad built a roaring fire in the fireplace, and Mom brought in marshmallows to roast. We children stood near the fire warming ourselves and our marshmallows and listening to the wind blowing around the corners of the house. Then we turned on the radio and waited for our favorite program to begin.

   We hadn't waited long, however, when there was a knock at the door.

Name_____

Using Transitions

What is your day like? Do you have chores to do?
Are there parts of your day that you really enjoy
and other parts that you would rather not have? Write
about your day, and use transitions between thoughts
to make your writing flow. Be sure to title your work.

It's Time to Write . . . Creative Writing

Writing is a form of expression much like painting or music, and people who do creative writing are truly artists.

Creative writing does not usually depend upon research or facts. It is often "made up" out of our own feelings and experiences. It may take the form of a poem; a short story; an essay or a new, unnamed form.

Creative writing is a right-brain activity for the most part. Of course, after the idea is created, you will use the left brain to develop it into a logical form.

The following example illustrates the difference between factual writing and creative writing.

Factual: A 90-mile-per-hour wind whipped through Cloud City yesterday upsetting trash cans and stirring up large clouds of dust.

Creative: The wind charged with a rush, like a band of thousands of troopers, each with his gun spitting particles of dust into the air.

Name_____

Factual or Creative?

Read each of the following selections, and decide if it is more factual or creative.

1. _____ A great horned owl has excellent hearing. It can detect a faint sound from a distance equal to half a city block.

2. _____ Mary's raccoon Ranger loved to play in the water. First, he hid behind the sofa and peeked out to see if Mary was watching, and then he scampered to his bowl and used his tiny hands to splash and splash. At first, Mary thought he was washing his food, but when she saw Ranger's big furry tail flipping back and forth, she knew that he was just having a good time!

3. _____ The hummingbird has a tiny bill that works much like a straw. When the bird finds a flower with nectar, he reaches his bill deep inside the flower and sucks.

4. _____ Rat-a-tat-tat. Rat-a-tat-tat-tat-tat! The woodpecker is working again! He uses his long, strong bill to find grubs under the bark of the tree. Oh! Cover your ears! There he goes again!

Rewrite the following factual selection to make it creative.

5. Today is a nice day.

_____

_____

_____

Practice Creative Writing

Artists are inspired to paint by seeing a beautiful scene or hearing music. What inspires you to write?

Think about each of the following phrases, and write your first reaction. If any of them inspire you to write a longer piece, write freely without thinking about spelling or correctness.

1. a small kitten crying for its mother

_____

_____

_____

2. the red, white and blue flag waving slowly in the breeze

_____

_____

_____

3. a toddler shaking hands with an old woman in a wheelchair

_____

_____

_____

4. a robin tugging on a huge nightcrawler

_____

_____

_____

Name _____

Poetry is a way of expressing yourself so that other people can share your view of the world. Good poetry has universal appeal–that is, many people can understand the meaning of the poem and share in the experience that the poet provides.

Poems have many different structures. The structure of a poem should match the subject matter.

One of the more beautiful forms of poetry was developed by the Japanese. Known as **haiku**, this poetry is made up of three lines. The first line has five syllables. (A syllable is a sound containing a vowel.) The second line has seven syllables, and the last line has five syllables.

Example: A baby's soft coo
brings indescribable joy
to his mother's heart.

Example: Slim, shiny fingers
of teasing, playful sunlight
reach for the ocean.

Now it's your turn! Think about something beautiful, and write a haiku verse about it.

_____

_____

_____

_____

96

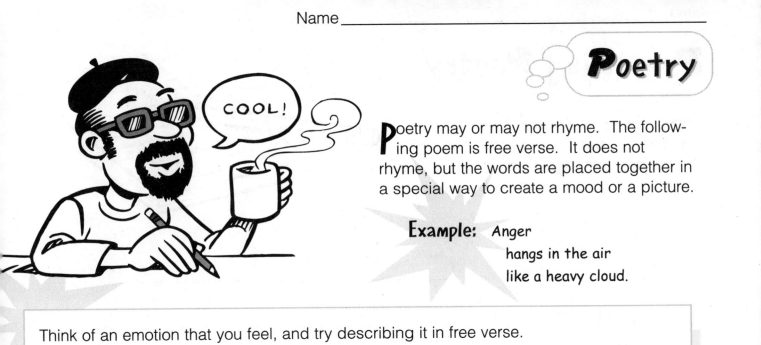

Poetry

COOL!

Poetry may or may not rhyme. The following poem is free verse. It does not rhyme, but the words are placed together in a special way to create a mood or a picture.

Example: Anger
hangs in the air
like a heavy cloud.

Think of an emotion that you feel, and try describing it in free verse.

_____

_____

_____

Some people enjoy writing humorous verse. One form of humorous verse is the limerick.

Example: A fellow with clothes very smart
Said that he could win any girl's heart.
Said he, "I'm so fine–
For me they all shine!"
Then he sat, and his pants split apart!

Try your luck at writing a limerick. Notice that the first two lines rhyme with the last line and that the third and fourth lines rhyme with each other.

_____

_____

_____

_____

Practicing Poetry

Try writing your own poetry.
You may use the examples
on the previous page for style,
or you may develop your own.

_____

_____

_____

_____

_____

_____

_____

_____

_____

_____

_____

_____

_____

_____

The Short Essay

Writers often use the essay form to express an opinion or to give their readers another way to look at something. An essay is a short discussion about one special topic.

The essay has an **opening**, a **body** and an **ending**.

Opening →

Body →

Ending →

My Family

I always used to think that my family was just my mother and father and brother and sister and me. We lived together and did things together and took care of each other.

As I grew up, I learned that my family was also my grandparents and uncles and aunts and cousins. We didn't live together, but sometimes we did things together, and we all cared about and helped each other when we could.

I noticed that some of the people in my family seemed to love each other, and some of them argued a lot, but all of them were still part of the same family. Even though they argued, they still cared about and helped each other.

Now that I am older, I believe that my family is really much larger. I believe that it includes everyone on Earth. We don't live together, and we don't do things together, but if we care about each other and help each when we can, the world will be a better place.

Name_____

Practice Writing a Short Essay

Are you concerned about keeping our air and water clean or about helping people to understand one another? Choose a topic that interests you, and write a short essay about it. Remember to think about the topic and brainstorm for ideas before you begin writing.

Although you do not need to use a formal outline for this essay, remember that your ideas must be in a logical order for your reader to follow them easily.

_____

_____

_____

_____

_____

_____

_____

_____

_____

_____

_____

_____

100

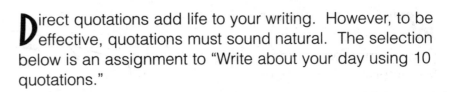

Direct quotations add life to your writing. However, to be effective, quotations must sound natural. The selection below is an assignment to "Write about your day using 10 quotations."

My Day

6:00	"Crummy alarm clock–it went off too early again!"
7:00	"Are we out of milk?"
9:00	"Sure, I'll be happy to run an errand for you."
10:00	"Do you have an extra pencil?"
11:00	"I'm starting to get hungry. How about you?"
12:00	"You're going to the Rockies game?"
1:00	"We have to write three pages–three pages!"
3:00	"I'll race you to the corner."
5:00	"Oh, school was okay. We have to write three pages for history."
7:00	"Okay! I'll be right over."

Did you notice that each quotation begins and ends with quotation marks? The end punctuation for a quotation goes inside the marks.

When a quotation is a part of a sentence, the end punctuation goes inside the marks unless the sentence is a question or an exclamation.

Examples: She asked, "Do I have enough money?"

Did she say, "I have enough money"?

The 10-Sentence Day

Write your own version of the 10-sentence day. Remember to keep the natural sound in your quotations.

_____

_____

_____

_____

_____

_____

_____

_____

_____

_____

_____

_____

_____

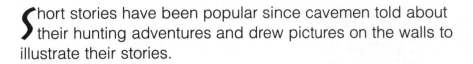

Short stories have been popular since cavemen told about their hunting adventures and drew pictures on the walls to illustrate their stories.

Good short stories start with a "grabber" opening that presents some kind of problem to be solved. The body of the story tells how the main characters deal with the problem. Following the body of the story is the climax, or high point, of the story. Often the climax ends the story, but some stories have a short ending following the climax.

The Big One

Opening—Conflict between Ben & Bryan

"My younger brother Ben fibs quite a lot," Bryan laughed, shoving the telephone a little closer against his ear. "I mean, he really tells some whoppers! I try to cover for him some of the time, but there's only so much a guy can do . . . Well, anyway, are you ready to go camping with us tomorrow? Bring your sleeping bag and canteen and your camera. We'll try to get some scenic shots."

Bryan hung up the phone, shaking his head at the memories of some of his brother's wild tales.

"I heard you talking to Dan," Ben yelled as he came stomping into the room. "I don't lie anymore, and you know it."

"Oh, don't get bent out of shape, Ben," Bryan laughed. "You just have more imagination than most of us. That's all!"

Just then Mr. Richards, the boys' father, came into the room. "Are you boys arguing?" he asked.

Body

"Oh, Ben's just hot 'cause I told Dan what big whoppers he tells."

"I don't! Not anymore!" Ben screamed.

"Ben used to have a problem, but he doesn't anymore," said Mr. Richards quietly. "I want you to leave him alone, Bryan."

The next morning Mr. Richards, Ben, Bryan and Bryan's friend Dan left to go camping. "There are big mountain lions in these mountains," Ben told Dan. "BIG ones! I read about them at school."

"Sure, Ben," Dan replied, winking at Bryan. "I'll watch out for them, and I'll take a picture of every lion I see."

"It's the truth, Dan," Ben insisted. "I did used to lie some, but I'm growing up now, and I don't do that anymore. You'd better believe me."

When evening came, there were two tents in the clearing. Bryan and Dan were in one tent, and Mr. Richards and Ben were in the other. "You know," said Bryan grinning, "with a flashlight and a few sound effects, we could make Ben think he was seeing a really BIG lion . . ."

"One BIG mountain lion coming up!" Dan agreed, and they slipped outside and began the show. Bryan yowled and growled, and Dan made big shadows appear on the wall of the tent that Ben and Mr. Richards were sharing.

It didn't take long for Ben to react. "Dad! Dad!" Ben screamed. "Look, it's a mountain lion! I just heard him and looked up–there!" Ben was wide-eyed.

"Hmm," said Mr. Richards thoughtfully. "Noisy one, isn't it? I kind of think there might even be TWO mountain lions . . . right, Bryan and Dan?" he answered, raising his voice.

By this time, Bryan and Dan were doubled up with laughter, and now they were roaring. "Dad! Dad! It's a mountain lion!" they mocked Ben in high squeaky voices. "Ha! Ha! There are no mountain lions within a hundred miles of here!"

The next morning just after breakfast, Bryan was on his way to get water when he noticed a set of large fresh tracks just a few feet away from the campsite. "Dan," he called when he returned with the water. "Come here a minute, will you?"

When they were just out of Ben's hearing, Bryan spoke in a husky voice. "There are some big tracks over here. Look at these!" The boys stood a moment studying the tracks.

Just then Mr. Richards and Ben came toward the boys. What are you looking at?" asked Mr. Richards, kneeling down to get a closer look.

Climax →

"Boys," Mr. Richards looked at Bryan and Dan. "These are mountain lion tracks, and they aren't very old. That lion must have been pretty hungry to come that close to human beings. Then he looked up at Ben, "Son, we really did have a mountain lion in camp last night!"

Bryan and Dan looked at each other sheepishly, while Ben grinned from ear to ear. "Say, Dad," Ben asked, "could we take a picture of those tracks? I'd kind of like to have a picture of them on the wall in my room—just as a reminder."

The End

Practice Writing a Short Story

Use your right brain (imagination) to think about the story you will write. When you have something in mind, answer the following questions to get started. Then write the story.

1. Who are the main characters?

   _____

2. Where does the story take place?

   _____

3. What is the problem to be solved?

   _____

   _____

4. How will the problem be solved?

   _____

   _____

5. How will the story open?

   _____

   _____

6. How will the story end?

   _____

   _____

7. What is the name of the story?

   _____

Name _____

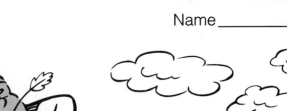

Review

For each exercise below, use the suggestion to improve the sentence.

1. Use specific nouns.

The man was very tall.

_____

2. Use descriptive verbs.

Henry looked at the map.

_____

3. Use interesting modifiers.

My friend painted the picture.

_____

4. A pronoun must refer to a specific noun.

Bret and Larry cleaned *his* room.

_____

5. Sentences of equal value can be combined with a comma and *and*, *but* or *or*.

My uncle would not let me use his camera. He would let me use his VCR.

_____

6. Sentences may be combined using subordinating conjunctions such as *if*, *when*, *since* and *because*.

Jerry sold the truck. It used too much gasoline.

_____

Name _____

This is a fountain of descriptive verbs. The more descriptive verbs you can think of, the higher the fountain.

Example:

study

observe

peek

watch

look

See how high you can make the fountain.

_____

_____

_____

_____

_____

_____

_____

_____

_____

_____ walk _____

108

Name _____

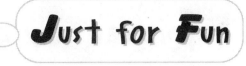

There are a number of pairs of words in the English language that sound alike but have different spellings and different meanings. An example is the pair *so* and *sew*. *So* tells us to what degree something happens as in "I like this *so* much!" *Sew* is a way of putting two pieces of cloth together.

Can you guess what these pairs of words are?

1. Shaking one's head from side to side   _____

Being aware of something   _____

2. The ocean   _____

To look   _____

3. A piece of clothing   _____

What you might say to chase away a bothersome fly   _____

4. What a ball might do   _____

The part an actor plays   _____

5. Hair on a horse's neck   _____

The most important one   _____

Supplementary Activities

Giving directions: tell how to follow a recipe, build a model airplane or any other step-by-step process.

Reporting an Event to a Newspaper: Write about a club meeting or social event and be certain to include who, what, where, when and why in the first sentence of the report. Arrangement of information is most important to least important with the newspaper sometimes cutting off a paragraph or two at the end.

Thank-You Notes: Write a thank-you note for an occasion when you have been to dinner, an overnight guest, given presents, etc.

Writing an Order: Complete an order form or write a letter to order materials by mail.

Minutes for a Meeting: Practice taking notes during a group meeting such as 4-H, Scouts or youth group.

Have a Family Game: The student writes the beginning of a story and folds down the edges of the paper. The family members know who the characters are but do not know what he has written. Each person adds to the story. Read what you have after everyone has had a turn.

Interview your parents, grandparents and other adults about their childhood experiences. What chores did they do? What did they do for fun? How much homework did they have? How were their lives different from yours? How were they the same?

Make your own movie on paper. Use two paper towel rolls to make a scroll. Write a story and illustrate it. Tape the illustrations together into a long roll and attach to the rolls.

Make a travel guide for your area. What would a visitor like to see? Give directions for getting there.

Develop a new game and write directions for it.

Set up your own writing center with a pen or pencil, dictionary, paper, table space and a folder or notebook for your finished work. You might want to keep special magazines or books you enjoy there, too.

Save your creative writing in a special notebook or scrapbook. Decorate it as you like. You may want to buy plastic sheets to put over your pages.

Are you an artist? Illustrate your work. Write a description, and draw a picture of what you have described.

Write a poem for a special occasion–a friend's birthday, your parents' anniversary, etc.

Keep a daily journal of what you do.

Use your writing skills to do special reports on things that interest you. Do you want to know more about people in another country? Are you curious about another planet?

Would you like to see your writing in print? Many children's magazines will accept submissions. Do remember, though, that most magazines receive many more submissions than they can use, and they must choose only those submissions that fit their available space.

Write a family newsletter, and send it to friends and family. You might find a friend or cousin who would like to help you.

Write a story, and read it to a younger brother or sister.

Put your best work on the refrigerator with magnets.

See the world differently. How would the world look if you were a very tall person? What would be different? Suppose you had super hearing or super vision? How would your world be different?

Try writing as you listen to music. Just write anything that comes to your mind for five minutes. Then repeat the exercise using a different kind of music. Do you see any difference in your writing?

Design a simple word puzzle or crossword puzzle. Use a theme such as Pets or Holidays.

Page 11

Group Sports: bowling, volleyball, baseball, track
Individual Sports: hang gliding, tennis, hiking, track
Answers will vary.
1. Most forms of transportation in the 1800s were pretty slow.
2. Today we travel at super speeds.

Page 13

1. toe! After, 2. everything?" "I, 3. tons. The,
4. water. The, 5. voice. "Can

Page 15

1. Watching birds feed their babies is fun.
2. Some of the best parts of a vacation . . . home.
3. This is an excellent picture!
4. Sandy visited three states on her vacation.
5. In the early evening, Joe heard the cries of the wild animals.

Page 16

1. The wild horse bucked in every direction.
2. Kerri introduced Jeff to all of her relatives.
3. It rained every day for a week.

Page 17

1. The President explained his plans.
2. Mary found four new friends.
3. Each child brought a storybook.
4. When I awakened, I saw the five children.
5. Barret gave us a tour.

Page 20

1. least to most: 1, 3, 4, 2; 2. spatial: 1, 4, 2, 3;
3. time: 1, 3, 2, 4; 4. time: 1, 4, 3, 5, 2

Page 25

1. return address, 2. date, 3. greeting, 4. body,
5. closing, 6. signature

Page 29

Bob Brooks
337 Overton Road
New City, OH 87777

Mr. Galen George
1500 Willow Lane
Anytown, CO 80666

Page 33

1. thinking
2. Who are you? Who is your reader? What do you want to say?
3. You need good ideas, and you don't want to leave anything out.
4. Arrange ideas under a main topic.
5. idea

Page 34

1. return address, 2. date, 3. inside address,
4. greeting, 5. message, 6. asking for a response,

7. closing, 8. signature
Just for Fun: Use your noodle.

Page 35

Doc, Jocko, Fuzz

Page 41

#2 summarizes the story best, #1 does not tell why they had to stop. #3 leaves out information about Anna and her father.

Page 43

"When" is missing from the report.

Page 44

Answers may vary.
A. 2, 1, 5, 3, 4   B. 2, 1, 4, 3

Page 45

Story 1: What was the contest?
Story 2: What kind of accident was it? Who was in it?

Page 47

Answers will vary.
1. Boy Wants License to Fly
2. Dinosaur Discovered Near Denver
3. Judd Joins Fast-Food Chain

Page 50

1. summary, 2. opinion, 3. author, 4. most,
5. first, 6. action, 7. missing

Page 59

1. a, 2. b, 3. b, 4. a, 5. b
Answers will vary.
1. More than half a million people have chosen to have a cat as a pet.
2. Did you know that an anthill is like a little community?
3. Did you know that bananas grow upside down?
4. If a fast-food chain sells two million hamburgers, what happens to all of the wrappers?
5. Last year John Elway made $3 million.

Page 61

1. People use different forms of transportation to get to work–cars, trains and ferries.
2. Dogs help police officers, fire fighters and rescue teams.
3. Artists show their talents by weaving, by drawing murals and by doing chain saw sculpting.
4. People can get the news from television, from the newspaper or from an on-line service.
5. The flours from many different grains can be used to make food.

Page 62

1. spatial, 2. step-by-step, 3. time order,
4. order of importance, 5. order of importance

Answer Key

Page 64

1. Crane, Stephen. <u>The Red Badge of Courage</u>. Pocket Books, Inc., 1954, p. 37.
2. Smolowe, Jill. "Shadow Play," <u>Time</u>. May 23, 1994, pp. 32-34.
3. King, Martin Luther. Speech in Washington, D.C., August 28, 1963.

Number 1 would be first, number 3 second.

Page 70

1. Rajah and the Rainbow Bird
2. Some people . . . than people.
3. Indian elephants are honored for their spirit. Indian elephants are honored for their ability to carry very heavy loads. Indian elephants are honored for their high intelligence.
4. last

Page 73

Answers will vary.

1. Ann looked at the hotel.
2. A sea gull hovered over Ann.
3. Ann and I fed the sea gull.
4. Ann and I watched the bird fly away.
5. Ann waved to the gull.

Page 76

1. The fire fighter helped John.
2. The police officer chased the dog.
3. I ate the apple.
4. Susan sent the letter.
5. The police officer caught the thief.
6. The old woodcutter built the fire.

Page 78

Answers will vary.

1. chewed-up, 2. odd-shaped, 3. creaky, 4. whiny, 5. young, 6. grocery, 7. wooden, 8. brand-new, 9. prize

Page 79

Answers will vary.

1. in my story, 2. under the bed, 3. beside the chair, 4. near the table, 5. on the dresser

Page 81

Answers will vary.

1. here, 2. now, 3. quickly, 4. silently, 5. there, 6. Later, 7. Now, 8. boldly, 9. there

Page 82

1. into the kitchen (where)
2. inside the refrigerator (where)
3. for several minutes (to what extent)
4. with great enthusiasm (how)
5. After her search (when); to bed (where)

Page 84

She was holding a letter in her hand, and she was very excited. "I got a letter from Aunt Jo, and she wants me to spend the summer with her! We can swim, and we can go horseback riding every day.

Page 85

1. Joseph held the donkey, and he watched it eat.
2. The donkey had a heavy load, but he didn't seem to mind it.
3. Joseph may keep the donkey, or he may sell it.
4. Joseph has a wagon for the donkey, but the wagon needs to be fixed.
5. The wagon is small, and it can hold only one person.

Page 87

When Barry came home from Jack's house because he had to do his chores.
If I tell you
"If you would like to tell me
"Since you're willing to think about it

1. Because I was late getting home, I missed dinner.
2. After the game ends, we can start a fire in the fireplace.
3. If I had a new bicycle, I could deliver newspapers.

Page 88

Answers may vary.

1. If Jack hid behind the stack of hay, no one would find him.
2. Because he heard someone coming, he crouched down low.
3. When the hay tickled Jack's nose, he sneezed.
4. When the sheriff walked into the barn, he heard Jack sneeze.
5. Because the sheriff laughed, Jack came out of his hiding place.

Page 91

1. Then, Finally
2. peace . . . Peace
3. Although Jose enjoyed being in the choir, . . .
4. cold
5. Then, waited

Page 94

1. factual, 2. creative, 3. factual, 4. creative

Page 109

1. no, know; 2. sea, see; 3. shoe, shoo; 4. roll, role; 5. mane, main

112